# Dancing Mind.
# Thinking Heart.

## Kru Harale

BookLeaf Publishing

India | USA | UK

Dancing Mind. Thinking Heart. © 2022

Kru Harale




Presentation by *BookLeaf Publishing*

Web: www.bookleafpub.com

E-mail: info@bookleafpub.com

ISBN: 9789357444668

First edition 2022

# DEDICATION

To every dancing mind and thinking heart.

# ACKNOWLEDGEMENT

I am eternally grateful to my friends and family, who are a constant source of joy and inspiration.

# Dancing mind, thinking heart.

When the intuition speaks,
in the language of art,
I listen carefully,
and paint my part.

On a canvas that talks,
loud and clear,
for everyone,
who wants to hear...

The voice inside,
inside the art,
Don't quieten its mind,
and thinking heart.

# Work in Progress

Don't judge my actions, let me speak today.
I might be wrong, in many ways,

But I still learn, I still grow,
into someone I wasn't before.

Getting better each day,
Bidding goodbye to old ways.

This goes on till the end,
Because we are a 'Work in Progress'

# Above the Sky

A happy sky, I see today
smiling wide at me, it says,
"I have the sun, the wind, the rain,
what do you want to experience today?"

I close my eyes and think aloud,
"I wish I could fly above this ground,
above the sun, the wind, the rain,
to be with you, staring down at Earth's face."

# Hopeful Heart

Sometimes all you need is a fresh start,
Because things aren't going as you thought.
Please hold on, and keep moving on,
"You're almost there" says your hopeful heart.

# Moving on...

And then I feel a bit confused.
Where do I belong? How can I be strong?
Going nowhere, I'm still moving on.

Onto a new reality that  I'll call it 'mine'
Searching for friends, who are true,
good, and kind.
They'll help me survive,
they'll help me be strong
They'll make me feel alive,
I'll call them 'mine'

Then I wish, I never belonged,
because goodbyes feel so wrong.
Moving on again, to another chapter.
which will end sooner or later.

# Everyday Gifts

We think its bad,
we think its blue,
we don't know it,
we just think it's true.

Let's look around
and really see.
Let's re-think,
what we believe.

Because life gives us gifts
every single day,
Let's open our eyes
and appreciate.

# Moment

A moment lost in time,
becomes a distant memory,
and helps us survive.
As we go through life,
learning lessons that guide,
in our journey through each moment,
the little moments,
that make our LIFE.

# Leave your Trail

Behold, my friends,
Fire away!
Take charge,
make your own way.
Leave your trail,
for another soul,
someday like you,
seeking their goal.

# Wonderful Affirmations

*(Adapted from "The Game of Life and How to Play It" by Florence Scovel Shinn)*

I do wonderful work,
in a wonderful way.
with wonderful people,
every wonderful day.
I give wonderful service,
for wonderful pay.

# Dark to Light

When I see the darkness, I know it'll go.
It'll fade away soon for something bright.
And then we'll know
The darkness, in fact, was the way to the light.

We only have to trust the path,
Because it always brings the joys we need.
Things are always going right.
even if they appear 'wrong' for the time being.

# Manifesting Life

The life we saw,
is the life that's here.
The life we seek,
is the life that's near.

# The Raining Sky

The sky cries for us to see,
that no soul has lived without misery.
Then the sun shines brightly, the very next day,
and we wonder at this beautiful mystery.

The oh so empty sky above,
taught us things we need to learn,
For after every night, comes the light.
After every rain, comes sunshine.

# Speak your heart

I asked the divine master above,
"What's the difference between you and me?
How do you live in harmony?
With so many sorrows going around.
How do you manage to sing out loud?"

They responded in a calming voice,
"We explore our sorrows and seek the divine,
As the truth unfolds with intuitive rhymes,
We only listen to life's advice,
to speak our hearts, and not our mind!"

# Reaching our Goal

Afraid of the truth, don't ever be,
It's the only way to be free.
We are blessed with every soul,
Helping us reach our goal.

# Architecture Speaks

*(This is something I wrote while visiting Bhuj,
Gujarat, India. An earthquake hit Gujarat in
2001, causing dilapidation of some very rich,
historic heritage structures)*

If buildings could talk, about their design,
I wonder if they'd want to change a line.
May be they aren't happy with their facade,
As the architect drew it,
coz it was easy on AutoCAD.

If the buildings could talk, they'd tell me the
goof-ups in construction,
and how it all added to the corruption!
Towers complaining
about the pollution in the city,
"We can't breathe", they say,
"with the environment so dirty!"

Choked with plaster and outlets only for ACs,
The buildings are suffocated,
please let in some breeze.
The heritage buildings have a different story,
Some boasting of royalties,
some basking in glory.

Some others, still manage to stand,
Crying out loud, but no helping hand.
If these buildings could talk,
I wouldn't need a tour guide,
the walls would tell me,
how they were built and why!

They would tell me history,
they would tell me tales,
And why their once rich coloured walls,
have now turned pale.

If buildings could talk, people would realize,
Architecture goes beyond space and time.
Actually, if buildings spoke,
I don't think it would matter,
Because people don't have an ear for each other.

I wish they'd just listen,
to what the buildings had to say,
Coz Architecture speaks anyway!!

# Why

Days go by,
with you on my mind,
I wonder why,
when you're not even mine.

# A Sad Day

With a teardrop floating in the eye,
I question Life,
"Why are there sad days,
which become memories,
making a heart heavy?"

Comes the response from Life,
"It always gets better with time,
once you let go, is the advice.
Then looking forward to a new way,
wiser and stronger because of a sad day"

# Believe in your dreams

Believe it's true,
Believe its real,
Coz once your through,
The good times will be here.
For all to enjoy,
for all to say,
Believe its new,
every passing day.

# Time Flies

Time flies by oh so soon,
Before we know it, we are gone,
To a brand new place than before,
reflecting on the memories galore.

# Everyday starts
# a New Year

Starting the new year with a lovely day,
Learning from our old mistakes,
Not denying them, but being true,
They did happen. They happened to better you.

If yesterday things didn't go your way,
With this new day, better times await.
So let's welcome the New Year, being true,
It will happen again. It will happen to better you.

# Goodnight Universe

*(I was taught this prayer in school)*

Goodnight Universe, I am going to bed,
work is over, prayers are said.
I am not afraid of this night,
for you will be watching over me
till morning light.

Thank you Universe!